after

A 30 DAY DEVOTIONAL HELPING RESTORE
HOPE AFTER THE STORMS OF LIFE

after

A 30 DAY DEVOTIONAL HELPING RESTORE
HOPE AFTER THE STORMS OF LIFE

Presented To

———————————————————————

From

———————————————————————

Date

———————————————————————

TABLE OF CONTENTS

DEDICATION

To all the volunteers who relentlessly serve in the worst of conditions in the worst of times, to deliver the greatest news ever given to all mankind!

To the Divine Wonder for all He has done, all He is doing, and those things yet to come!

To those who feel like all hope is lost, at the end of their road, entrenched in doubt, worry, and fear; may the God of all Hope bring you peace through His precious promises!

HOPE FOR HARD TIMES

Scripture has much to say about hard times. These 30 days of personal devotionals are rooted in the Bible. They offer what Scripture always gives: help, comfort, wisdom, encouragement, hope and other spiritual resources for coping with life's challenges.

Some of the same subjects are addressed on multiple days. This is because we need to hear these messages over and over in life.

These devotionals contain universal truths, but they are written for *you*.

Texans on Missions brings help, hope and healing to people in many challenging situations. Our volunteers provide physical acts of service and comfort for the people they serve.

We developed these devotionals with the people we serve – you – in mind. We wanted to leave you with some of God's truth when we can no longer be with you.

We all need to be connected with other followers of Christ. We need a church, some of which are now called fellowships. Both "church" and "fellowship" are rooted in Scripture. God knew we needed to not be alone in our faith journey.

These devotionals are written from the firm belief that every person needs a trusting relationship with God through Jesus Christ.

If you have never made such a decision to follow Christ, a local church or fellowship can help you understand what this means. You can use these daily devotionals as a starting point. You will see how God helps people in tough situations. They will begin to open insights into the great blessings available to those who follow Christ on both the good days and the bad ones.

If you have already made a faith decision for Christ, we hope these devotionals help you deepen your faith. No believer has walked perfectly with Christ. Scripture is clear: We all have sinned – messed up in life. But God is there to help us with each new day as we seek to serve Him better. Every new day is a new start.

Day 1

AS YOU KNOW, LIFE CAN BE DIFFICULT

Genesis 39:2–3, 21, 23: The Lord was with Joseph so that he prospered, and he lived in the house of his Egyptian master. When his master saw that the Lord was with him and that the LORD gave him success in everything he did, ...the LORD was with him; he showed him kindness and granted him favor in the eyes of the prison warden. ...

The warden paid no attention to anything under Joseph's care, because the LORD was with Joseph and gave him success in whatever he did."

The Bible contains many stories of God's encounters with men and women. These verses from Genesis tell about Joseph, one of the great heroes of Scripture.

Joseph's story is interesting. It extends from the heights of his achievements to the depths of his disappointment.

Joseph is recorded as having the **constant** favor and blessing of God, yet he is continually plagued with hardships and difficulties. Still, we are reminded over and over that the Lord was, with, Joseph.

God doesn't always remove the obstacles and circumstances causing hardships in our life. That may not sound comforting. But God will grant you favor and peace in the middle of whatever you are going through.

How do we respond when, instead of deliverance, God requires endurance?

The real beauty of Joseph's story is not in the astounding deliverance God provides, but rather in His unwavering and consistent care of Joseph during his darkest hours.

God never abandoned Joseph. He remained with him and blessed him throughout his life, even when his prayers were left unanswered for long stretches of time.

Today, God can be sufficient for you even in the middle of tough circumstances. Whatever comes, God wants to walk with you as He did with Joseph. Seek God's glory and His purposes, as Joseph did, and the blessings will come for you and for others.

NOTES

Day 2

GOD IS WITH YOU

Isaiah 41:10: *"So do not fear, for I am with you; do not be dismayed, for I am your God. I will strengthen you and help you; I will uphold you with my righteous right hand."*

In a world that often feels chaotic and uncertain, there is an unshakable truth that brings us comfort and hope: God is with us. The promise of God's presence is not a mere platitude; it is a profound reality that can transform our lives.

Everything may not be ok, but if God is with you, you will be ok.
– Mark Driscoll

Isaiah 41:10 reminds us of God's reassuring words: "So do not fear, for I am with you." These words are an invitation to lay aside our anxieties and apprehensions, for in God's presence, fear finds no fertile ground to grow.

In our loneliest moments, we are never truly alone.

In our weakest moments, we are strengthened by His presence.

In our darkest moments, we are guided by His light.

God doesn't merely stand beside us as a passive observer. He is actively engaged in our lives, offering strength when we are weak, help when we are in need and guidance when we are lost. His presence is not distant; it is an ever-present, unwavering support.

Today, take a moment to reflect on the profound truth that God is with you.

- *In your joys and sorrows, successes and failures, He is there.*
- *In your moments of solitude and in your bustling days, His presence surrounds you.*
- *In your challenges and uncertainties, He is your anchor.*

Notes

Day 3

JOY COMES IN THE MORNING

Psalm 30:5b: *Weeping may stay for the night, but rejoicing comes in the morning.*

Sorrow is a heavy burden, one we all bear at some point in our lives. It casts a shadow over our hearts, leaving us feeling lost and overwhelmed. Yet, even in the darkest hours of sorrow, there is a promise of light and comfort in the words of Psalm 30.

There is a joy available that the deepest grief cannot put out. No circumstance or person can take away the joy God gives. - Timothy Keller

Like a long and tearful night, sorrow can seem endless. It often arrives uninvited, triggered by loss, disappointment or pain. It can feel as if joy has abandoned us, leaving behind a void that nothing can fill.

Somehow the sorrow we are facing latches onto us like a leech sucking life out of us minute by minute. Eventually the sorrow feels so overwhelming, so endless, we begin to believe it is permanent.

But Scripture reminds us that sorrow is not the end of the story, it's not the end of our stories.

This is not a permanent dwelling place. Instead, it is a season – a night that will eventually give way to a morning.

In the night of sorrow, we learn to lean on God in ways we never thought possible. We discover the depth of His compassion and the beauty of His grace.

God specializes in new beginnings.

Today, God offers you light even if everything seems dark. He offers joy even in the midst of sorrows. Your morning of rejoicing may not come immediately, but it will come. And in it you will find a renewed sense of hope, comfort and even deeper intimacy with the One who walks with you through the night.

NOTES

Day 4

GOD BRINGS YOU COMFORT

2 Corinthians 1:3-4: *Praise be to the God and Father of our Lord Jesus Christ, the Father of compassion and the God of all comfort, who comforts us in all our troubles so that we can comfort those in any trouble with the comfort we ourselves receive from God.*

G od is not only our source of comfort; He is the very essence of comfort itself. He is "the God of all comfort," and His compassion knows no bounds.

"Listen to God with a broken heart. He is not only the doctor who mends it, but also the father who wipes away the tears."
- Criss Jami

When we are in distress, God does not stand at a distance. He draws us near with arms open wide, ready to envelop us in His loving embrace.

The beauty of divine comfort is that ...

◆ it goes beyond surface-level consolation,

◆ it reaches into the depths of our souls to touch the places where we hurt the most, and

◆ it whispers reassurance to our troubled hearts, reminding us that we are not alone in our struggles.

Yet, God's comfort doesn't stop with us. It has a purpose – a divine purpose. It equips us to be agents of comfort to others. Just as we receive comfort from God in our times of need, we are called to extend that same comfort to those who are hurting.

Today, in your journey through life's trials, remember that God is your constant source of comfort. Receive His comfort with an open heart and share it with others. Becoming a conduit of His love and grace in a world that longs for solace and hope.

NOTES

Day 5

You Can Move from Frustration to Faith

Psalm 13:1-6: How long, LORD? Will you forget me forever? How long will you hide your face from me? How long must I wrestle with my thoughts and day after day have sorrow in my heart? How long will my enemy triumph over me? Look on me and answer, LORD my God. Give light to my eyes, or I will sleep in death, and my enemy will say, "I have overcome him," and my foes will rejoice when I fall. But I trust in your unfailing love; my heart rejoices in your salvation. I will sing the LORD's praise, for he has been good to me.

Have you ever felt this way – that God has forgotten you?

Have you ever thought to yourself, "Where is God in the middle of all this? How long until He answers me?"

"Faith is taking the first step even when you can't see the whole staircase." — Martin Luther King, Jr.

In Psalm 13, David cries out to God in despair, questioning how long he must endure his hardships. He feels forgotten by God and oppressed by others. But even in his darkest moments, David does not give up on his faith. He turns to God for help and asks Him for the strength to carry on.

Throughout the Bible, we see examples of righteous people who grappled with anger and frustration toward God.

Job, for instance, endured immense suffering and questioned God's actions. Yet, even in his anger, Job maintained his faith and ultimately found healing and restoration through his unwavering trust in God's wisdom and goodness.

You may have similar feelings now. Doubt, anger, frustration. Know this: Through trusting God you can go through the same process as David in Psalm 13. You can move from frustration to faith.

Today, in the midst of life's struggles and uncertainty, remember that strength can be found in the Lord. Like David, you can cry out to God in your pain and ask for help. You can trust in the promises of His Word, knowing that He is with you always, even when you can't see or feel His presence.

NOTES

Day 6

It's Only a Chapter
in Your Story

Psalm 34:17-18: *The righteous cry out, and the LORD hears them; He delivers them from all their troubles. The LORD is close to the brokenhearted and saves those who are crushed in spirit."*

Life can take unexpected turns, and sometimes we find ourselves in the midst of a crisis – feeling overwhelmed, broken and unsure of what lies ahead. In such moments, it's essential to remember that we are not alone.

"The man who has God for his treasure has all things in One."
– A.W. Tozer

Psalm 34:17-18 assures us that when the righteous cry out, the Lord hears and delivers them from their troubles. And the New Testament says followers of Christ have been "made righteous" through Jesus' death and resurrection (Romans 5:1).

Also, the Lord is especially close to the brokenhearted and those who are crushed in spirit.

It's natural to question why we face such difficulties, but even in a crisis there is an opportunity for transformation. Crises have a way of stripping away the non-essentials and revealing what truly matters. It's in these moments of vulnerability that we can draw nearer to God and experience His presence in profound ways.

But how do we find hope in a crisis? It begins with acknowledging our need for God. We cry out to Him, not just with our words but with our hearts. This cry of surrender makes room for Christ's strength. In our weakness, God's strength is made perfect.

As you navigate this crisis, remember it is not the end of your story. A crisis is only a chapter; it is not the entire book. God is the author of your life, and He has plans to prosper you, even in the darkest of times.

Today, if you are in the midst of a crisis, you have an opportunity to experience God's faithfulness in a unique way. Trust that He hears your cries, that He is close to your broken heart, and that He will lead you through this storm into a brighter tomorrow. This crisis may shake you, but it cannot break you when you are anchored in the unwavering love of God.

NOTES

Day 7

REBUILDING YOUR LIFE

Nehemiah 2:17: Then I said to them, "You see the trouble we are in: Jerusalem lies in ruins, and its gates have been burned with fire. Come, let us rebuild the wall of Jerusalem, and we will no longer be in disgrace."

Life throws challenges our way, and they may leave us feeling as though we're standing amid the rubble of a once-thriving city. Our dreams, our plans and our hopes can crumble before us, leaving behind debris of disappointment and discouragement. Yet, in the midst of this rubble, there is a call to rebuild.

"The issue of faith is not so much whether we believe in God, but whether we believe the God we believe in." — R.C. Sproul

Nehemiah paints a vivid picture of a city in ruins. Jerusalem's walls have been broken down, and its gates have been burned with fire. It's a symbol of devastation, vulnerability and disgrace. But Nehemiah's response was not to wallow in despair; it was a call to action: "Come, let us rebuild."

Rebuilding is not only a physical endeavor; it's also a spiritual and emotional one. It's about restoring what has been lost, regaining what has been taken and renewing what has been broken. It's about rising from the ashes of adversity and rebuilding a life that stands strong and secure.

Rebuilding begins with a vision for what can be – a vision for renewal. It requires a willingness to acknowledge the brokenness and a determination to take the first steps toward the new vision.

If you find yourself surrounded by the ruins of your own dreams or the shattered pieces of your life, take heart. God is the master Rebuilder, and He specializes in transforming brokenness into beauty.

Nehemiah rallied the people to rebuild Jerusalem's walls by calling on God. We, too, can call on God's strength and guidance to rebuild your lives out of what has been lost.

Today, rise from the rubble. Take up the tools of faith and determination. And join in the divine work of rebuilding. In doing so, you'll find that God can bring beauty from the ashes and restoration from the ruins of life's challenges.

NOTES

Day 8

GOD OFFERS YOU PEACE
AS JESUS KNEW IT

John 14:27: *"Peace I leave with you; my peace I give you. I do not give to you as the world gives. Do not let your hearts be troubled and do not be afraid."*

In a world filled with noise, chaos and constant demands, the promise of peace is like a soothing balm for our weary souls. In John 14:27, Jesus offers a unique kind of peace; it's a peace that is different from a fleeting calm the world can provide.

God cannot give us a happiness and peace apart from Himself, because it is not there. There is no such thing. – C.S. Lewis

The peace that Jesus offers transcends even our most challenging circumstances. It's not just any peace; it's His peace. It's the same peace that allowed Him to sleep soundly in a boat tossed by raging waves. It's a peace that defies logic and reason because it is rooted in an unshakable trust in God.

How can you have such a peace? Is this type of peace truly available? Unequivocally, yes!

This peace is a gift, freely given to us by our Savior. It's a peace that surpasses understanding. When the world around us trembles, we can have an inner serenity that remains unmoved. It's a peace that allows us to navigate life's uncertainties with confidence, knowing that we are held by the One who calms the storms.

God is not distant, and He has not abandoned you. He is right there with you, providing strength, help and unwavering support. Place your confidence in His unwavering and mighty hands.

Today, you will not be able to control your circumstances, but you can choose to trust God. He loves you, is aware of your situation and can bring good from any circumstance.in the One who controls the storms themselves. Trust God to carry you through whatever you face today.

NOTES

Day 9

GOD KNOWS
YOU & YOUR PAIN

Psalm 139:1-4: *You have searched me, LORD, and you know me. You know when I sit and when I rise; you perceive my thoughts from afar. You discern my going out and my lying down; you are familiar with all my ways. Before a word is on my tongue you, LORD, know it completely."*

Have you ever felt completely overcome by the chaos of life?

To know that God knows everything about me and yet loves me is indeed my ultimate consolation.

- R. C. Sproul

Unexpected challenges, uncertainties and changes can leave us feeling unprepared and unsure how to move forward.

Our God is completely unfazed by the complexities of even our most chaotic situations. Your situation, no matter how surprising or bewildering it may be to you, is not a surprise to God.

In Psalm 139, David beautifully pronounces the depth of God's knowledge about us. God knows you inside and out, from the moments of stillness to the busiest of days. He knows your thoughts, your desires, your fears and your joys. Not only that; He's familiar with all your ways – your habits, your routines and even your peculiarities.

Now, here's the incredible part: God's knowledge of you isn't limited to your past or your present. He sees your future as well. He sees the path ahead, the challenges you'll face and the victories you'll celebrate. He's fully aware of what you're going through and what lies ahead. He's already equipped you with the strength, wisdom and grace you need for the journey.

Today, what does this mean for you? It means you can trust God no matter what. He is not caught off guard by the twists and turns of your life. He's with you, guiding you and providing for you. Embrace the peace that comes from surrendering your circumstances to the One who knows you best and loves you most.

NOTES

Day 10

WORRY GIVES WAY
WHEN YOU TRUST GOD

Matthew 6:25-27: "Therefore I tell you, do not worry about your life, what you will eat or drink; or about your body, what you will wear. Is not life more than food, and the body more than clothes? Look at the birds of the air; they do not sow or reap or store away in barns, and yet your heavenly Father feeds them. Are you not much more valuable than they? Can any one of you by worrying add a single hour to your life?"

Worry is a relentless companion in our daily lives. It creeps in like an unwelcome guest to steal our peace and cause turmoil within us. Yet, in the midst of our anxieties, Jesus offers us a profound perspective on worry.

Jesus encourages us to trade our worries for trust in God's care and faithfulness. Jesus reminds us that worry is not only useless; it's also harmful. It robs us of the joy and peace that come from trusting in God's goodness and faithfulness.

The heart of Jesus' message is a question that pierces through our worries: "Can any one of you by worrying add a single hour to your life?" Worry, though common, is ultimately unproductive. It doesn't solve problems or improve circumstances; it merely robs us of the joy and peace we could be experiencing.

Worry is, in essence, a lack of trust – a lack of trust in God's provision, His timing and His wisdom. It's a declaration that we believe our concerns are too great for God to handle. But here's the truth: God is not just capable of handling our worries; He invites us to cast them upon Him.

Today, release your burden of worry. Trade your anxious thoughts for trust in our heavenly Father. He knows your needs, and He cares deeply for you. When worry knocks at the door of your heart, remember the birds of the air and God's promise to provide what you need. Trust that His grace is sufficient and His peace surpasses understanding.

NOTES

Day 11

GOD HAS AN ANSWER FOR YOUR FEARS

Isaiah 41:10: *"So do not fear, for I am with you; do not be dismayed, for I am your God. I will strengthen you and help you; I will uphold you with my righteous right hand."*

Life often brings us uncertainty, difficulty and turmoil that threaten to overwhelm us. In such times, it is easy to become fearful, to think life is caving in around us

The presence of fear does not mean you have no faith. Fear visits everyone. But make your fear a visitor and not a resident.
- Max Lucado

What fears are shaking the foundations of your life? What circumstances are preventing you from moving forward?

Take heart, for during life's storms God offers a promise of hope and reassurance. God is most certainly, without a doubt, more than able.

In Isaiah 41:10, God speaks directly to our anxieties and fears. "Do not fear, for I am with you," He says. No matter how fierce the storm may be, God's presence is our anchor. He stands with us, unshaken, as a beacon of unwavering strength.

God is not a distant observer but a caring and sovereign God who knows every detail of our struggles. "I will strengthen you and help you." That's a promise from God.

In the face of life's tempests, God offers His divine strength. This all-powerful strength surpasses our own, enabling us to endure, persevere and even find moments of peace in the chaos.

Lastly, God declares, "I will uphold you with my righteous right hand." This image reminds us that God's support is unwavering. His right hand, a symbol of His power and favor, upholds us when we feel weak and vulnerable. His righteousness ensures that His help is just and perfect.

Today, remember God's words from Isaiah 41:10:

◆ *Do not fear.*
◆ *I am with you.*
◆ *Do not be dismayed.*
◆ *I am your God.*

- *I will give you strength.*
- *I will help you.*
- *I will uphold you.*

NOTES

Day 12

YOU COME NEAR
TO GOD WITH PRAYER

James 4:8a: *Come near to God and he will come near to you.*

Prayer is the sacred bridge connecting our hearts to God. It's a divine invitation to draw near to the Creator of the universe, to converse with Him and to experience His presence.

James beautifully encapsulates this truth: "Come near to God, and He will come near to you."

If your day is hemmed in with prayer, it is less likely to come unraveled.
— Cynthia Lewis

The Divine Wonder has issued an open invitation to converse with Him. Prayer is not a mere ritual or a religious duty; it's a personal encounter with the living God.

Prayer invites us to bring our joys, our sorrows, our hopes and our fears into God's presence. It's a place where we can pour out our hearts knowing we are heard and loved.

When we come to God in prayer, we acknowledge our dependence on Him. Prayer is not about eloquent words or religious formulas; it's about a genuine heart-to-heart conversation with God. He invites us to speak to Him openly, honestly and reverently. He invites us to lay our burdens before Him and to seek His guidance and wisdom.

It doesn't matter where you are or what you've done. God's arms are open wide to accept you. He is ready to meet you in the quiet of your heart, in the midst of life's chaos and in the stillness of your soul.

Today, draw near to God in prayer. Think of the time as sitting alone with a dearest friend, someone who loves you no matter the circumstances. Give the encounter some time, just as you give a good friend time. You'll discover that He draws near to you with His peace, His comfort and His presence. In prayer, you encounter the One who knows you deeply, loves you unconditionally and will guide you unfailingly.

NOTES

Day 13

PRAISE GOD EVEN IN YOUR TOUGH TIMES

Psalm 34:1: *I will extol the LORD at all times;*
his praise will always be on my lips.

This psalm sounds splendid, but let's be honest, the weight of life's pain and problems often leave us in putrid conditions.

How did the psalmist discover the transforming power of turning difficulties into praise?

Did the writer somewhere muster some unknown strength to sing and have a heart of thanksgiving? Or is there something else?

Praise and glory to God, for whom nothing is too hard. - Elisabeth Elliot

The author appears to know a much deeper truth – that praise does not depend on our circumstances but on our unwavering faith in God.

When we praise God in the midst of difficulties, we shift our focus from the problem to the Problem Solver. Praising God in difficulties is not about denying our struggles but about rising above them. Praise becomes a lifeline connecting us to God's grace and power.

Consider the story of Paul and Silas in prison (Acts 16:25-26). Despite their dire circumstances, they chose to sing praises to God. Their praise didn't just lift their own spirits; it resulted in a supernatural intervention – prison doors opened and chains broke.

Today, as you navigate your struggles, remember that praise is a lifeline that sustains you through tough times. When difficulties come, give God and watch how God transforms your heart, your perspective and even your circumstances. Praise turns difficulties into opportunities to experience the power and presence of the Almighty.

NOTES

Day 14

GOD IS PRESENT EVEN IN YOUR LONELINESS

Psalm 139:7-10: *Where can I go from your Spirit? Where can I flee from your presence? If I go up to the heavens, you are there; if I make my bed in the depths, you are there. If I rise on the wings of the dawn, if I settle on the far side of the sea, even there your hand will guide me, your right hand will hold me fast.*

You're not alone. You may feel lonely. You may even be experiencing loss, abandonment or isolation, but you are not deserted completely.

Sometimes you have to get to the place where He is all you have, to realize He is all you need
– Mikey Osborne

The psalmist penned words of solace and hope in Psalm 139. God's presence is not confined by time, space or circumstance. He is not distant. He is an ever-present, loving Father who walks with us through every season of life.

There is no place we can go, no depth we can sink to and no distance we can travel where God's presence cannot reach us.

Sometimes, like small children playing hide and seek, we feel we are hiding from God even when in plain sight. Circumstances, storms and even our own running cannot hide us from the God who is everywhere.

Jesus promises: "I am with you always, to the very end of the age" (Matthew 28:20b).

Today, remember you are never truly alone. God's presence is your constant companion. His love is your refuge. His hand is there to guide and hold you fast. Even in the depths of loneliness, you can find comfort in the unchanging presence of the One who knows you intimately and cares for you deeply.

NOTES

Day 15

CHALLENGES CAN TEACH
YOU TO PERSEVERE

Romans 5:3-4: Not only so, but we also glory in our sufferings, because we know that suffering produces perseverance; perseverance, character; and character, hope.

Perseverance is a quality forged in the crucible of life's challenges. It's the unwavering commitment to continue moving forward despite difficulties, setbacks and obstacles.

What saves a man is to take a step. Then another step. – C.S. Lewis

You persist. You keep on when things are hard.

And as you persevere, you become different. You are on the pathway to developing your character and building hope for your tomorrows.

When we face suffering, our natural inclination may be to avoid or escape them. But the Bible encourages us to "glory in our sufferings." This is hard to hear, but it's a perspective that views difficulties as opportunities for growth, not as insurmountable barriers.

Suffering has the capacity to produce perseverance. It's akin to the process of forging steel. The raw material is heated, hammered and shaped through intense heat and pressure.

Similarly, our character is refined and strengthened in the fires of adversity.

Ultimately, perseverance leads to hope. Hope is not wishful thinking; it's a confident expectation built on God's promises. It's the assurance that, regardless of our circumstances, God is at work, and He is writing a redemptive story through our lives.

Life's difficulties are opportunities for growth. They can teach us to persevere, if we let them. That improves our character. And that leads to hope.

Today, may your journey of perseverance be marked by faith, courage and an unwavering trust in God's faithfulness. As you press on, may you discover that even in the midst of life's struggles hope shines brightly to illuminate the path ahead.

NOTES

Day 16

JESUS OFFERS YOU AN
OVERCOMING FAITH

1 John 5:4: *... for everyone born of God overcomes the world. This is the victory that has overcome the world, even our faith.*

The path of life is riddled with barriers, tests and tribulations that can feel overwhelming at times. You have undoubtedly faced some and are battling some even now.

> *All the world is full of suffering. It is also full of overcoming. - Helen Keller*

Yet, in the midst of life's battles, we are called to be overcomers. John reminds us that everyone born of God overcomes the struggles of this world, and this victory is rooted in our faith.

Overcoming is *not* rooted in a survivalist mentality. It's rooted in a call to thrive despite the odds. It requires a mindset of resilience, an unwavering determination that you can face anything with God by your side.

Our source of overcoming power is Jesus Christ, through His life, death and resurrection. We access His power through faith in Jesus, who has already overcome the world.

When we face trials it's easy to be overwhelmed. Faith, however, reminds us that we serve a God who specializes in turning the impossible into the possible. It's a faith that sees the Red Sea before it parts and yet still trusts that God can part the waters for safe passage.

Today, remember the victory has already been won through Christ. Your faith is the key that unlocks access to the power to overcome. Trust that God is with you. With Him you can conquer any obstacle.

NOTES

Day 17

YOU CAN FIND
COMFORT IN GOD'S LOVE

Romans 8:38-39: *For I am convinced that neither death nor life, neither angels nor demons, neither the present nor the future, nor any powers, neither height nor depth, nor anything else in all creation, will be able to separate us from the love of God that is in Christ Jesus our Lord."*

God's love is unlike any other love we encounter in this world. It's a love so deep and so boundless that it defies human comprehension.

Isn't it a comfort to worship a God we cannot exaggerate? - Francis Chan

In Romans, Paul paints a vivid picture of the incomparable nature of God's love – a love that transcends time, space and circumstances.

Our human relationships, no matter how strong, can sometimes falter or fade. People may disappoint us, and circumstances may change. But God's love is unwavering, a constant presence in our lives that remains unshaken by the storms of life.

It's a love that embraces us in our darkest moments, whispers comfort in our pain and rejoices in our victories. When we are at our best and when we are at our worst, God's love remains steadfast, an unchanging force that surrounds us.

God's love is not conditional; it doesn't depend on our performance or merit. It's a love that chooses us, pursues us and redeems us. It's the love that sent Jesus to the cross, bearing our sins and securing our salvation.

Today, take a moment to imagine being immersed in God's love. Think of swimming in a gentle stream and what it feels like to be fully in the water's embrace. Let God's love wash over you, cleansing your doubts and fears. May you find comfort and assurance in the unbreakable bond of love that nothing in all creation can separate you from the all-encompassing love of God in Christ Jesus our Lord.

NOTES

Day 18

Cast Your Anxieties on God

---

1 Peter 5:6-10: *Humble yourselves, therefore, under God's mighty hand, that he may lift you up in due time. Cast all your anxiety on him because he cares for you. Be alert and of sober mind. Your enemy the devil prowls around like a roaring lion looking for someone to devour. Resist him, standing firm in the faith, because you know that the family of believers throughout the world is undergoing the same kind of sufferings. And the God of all grace, who called you to his eternal glory in Christ, after you have suffered a little while, will himself restore you and make you strong, firm and steadfast*

Sober-minded. Seeing life as it really is and living that life with focus. Sounds nice. But who in the world can be sober-minded in such a world as this?

You can!

"The beginning of anxiety is the end of faith, and the beginning of true faith is the end of anxiety."
~ George Mueller

With the many tasks we navigate each day and the schedules we keep, is it really possible to be sober-minded? It is an anxiety-producing world.

Experiencing anxiety seems to be the farthest thing from being sober-minded, and it also seems to be an epidemic of our time.

In the last decade, anxiety has overtaken depression as the number one reason people in the United States seek counseling. We can actually become addicted to worry and anxiety. And our brain can even learn to crave the sensation of worry.

There is, however, good news. Like any other bad habit, it can be broken.

If you are caught in a web of anxiety, it's OK to not be OK. But you do not have to remain in such a demanding and vile state.

Being sober-minded doesn't mean your schedule is clear of commitments; it simply means you are free from anxiety's intoxicating influences that would rob you of clear thinking. In other words, your mind is not clouded with thoughts of anxiety, depression and fear. Instead, you receive the freedom and hope that come from being a child of God.

Today, in the midst of life's stresses, ask God to help you approach the chaos with a sober mind – a mind that sees life for what it is and focuses on navigating it effectively. And, most importantly, set your mind on the things of Christ, the things of eternity. This eternal perspective conquers all momentary fears and worries.

NOTES

Day 19

You Find Rest
in God's Shelter

Psalm 91:1: *Whoever dwells in the shelter of the Most High will rest in the shadow of the Almighty.*

Amid the chaos of everyday life there lies a hidden sanctuary, a haven like no other. Psalm 91:1 invites us to dwell in the shelter of the Most High, finding rest in the shadow of the Almighty.

Thou hast created us for Thyself, and our heart is not quiet until it rests in Thee. - Augustine

What a remarkable promise. Can you imagine how great, mighty, majestic and impenetrable is the shelter of God? His shelter is readily available for those of us who seek it.

It is similar to securing housing – a place for our physical residence. We do not wait until a storm approaches before we seek a safe shelter. We prepare in advance. We rent or buy a place that gives us shelter even on the days when it is not needed.

But earthly shelters, of course, can be destroyed. But the covering protection of God cannot be wiped out. It remains in place even when things around us are in shambles, even when it *feels* like everything has been destroyed.

We access the shelter of God by sustaining a relationship over time. We make time for prayer, for reading His Word and for simply being still in His presence. We do this regularly, even when life is going well. Then, when the challenges come, God is like our most dependable friend, the one who walks closely with us when we feel hurt, alone and vulnerable.

A daily experience with God is like going to your own secret place with this most dependable friend. In this secret place you will discover a peace that surpasses understanding. You'll find strength to face challenges, and your fears will be quelled by the knowledge that the Almighty is with you.

Your secret place becomes a wellspring of faith, a source of hope, and a sanctuary of love.

It is best to find this spiritual shelter before troubles come, but it is never too late to seek it, even if you are not in the midst of the hardest of times.

Today, take a moment to close your eyes and envision yourself in a secret garden; it is the shelter of the Most High. No matter where you are or what you're facing, you can dwell there. In the midst of life's chaos find solace, rest, and the shadow of the Almighty. It's in this secret place that you'll discover the truest peace and the deepest love you've ever known.

NOTES

Day 20

GOD OFFERS YOU HOPE

Romans 15:13: *May the God of hope fill you with all joy and peace as you trust in him, so that you may overflow with hope by the power of the Holy Spirit.*

Hope is powerful. It can illuminate the darkest of nights and carry us through the stormiest seas of life.

Romans 15:13 tells us about the God of hope. He not only offers us hope but fills us with it. It then becomes possible to overflow with hope even in the most challenging of times.

Hope means expectancy when things are otherwise hopeless. - Gilbert K. Chesterton

God is an anchor for our souls, a source of joy and peace, and a wellspring of strength that empowers us to face life's trials with courage.

The God of hope invites us to trust in Him. It's in trusting Him that we find our joy and peace.

Trusting God means surrendering our fears, doubts and anxieties to Him, believing that He is in control and that His plans are filled with hope and purpose.

Hope is not merely wishful thinking or blind optimism. It's a confident expectation that God is at work, even when circumstances suggest otherwise. It's the assurance that He can turn the darkest chapters of our lives into stories of redemption and restoration.

Today, if you find yourself in despair or uncertainty, turn in prayer to the God of hope. Seek His presence and trust in His unfailing love. As you do, you'll discover your hope is not determined by your circumstances. Renewed hope will be empowered by God's Holy Spirit.

NOTES

Day 21

YOU NEED OTHERS TO LIVE WELL

Ecclesiastes 4:9-10: *Two are better than one because they have a good return for their labor: If either of them falls down, one can help the other up. But pity anyone who falls and has no one to help them up.*

Life is meant to be lived in community. We are wired for connection, designed to walk alongside others on our journey of faith and life. In Ecclesiastes, we are reminded of the beauty and importance of finding community – a partnership that brings mutual support, encouragement and strength.

In a world that can feel isolating and individualistic, the pursuit of genuine community is vital. It's not just about being in the company of others; it's about finding a place. It's a place

♦ where you belong,

♦ where you can grow and

♦ where you can contribute to the well-being of others.

God never intended for us to go through life alone. He created us to live in relationships – with Him and with others.

Finding community is not only about joining a group. It's about finding a spiritual family that points you to Christ and walks with you through the ups and downs of life.

Don't be afraid to reach out and build relationships. In community, you'll find a place where your gifts and talents can be used to bless others, and where you, too, will be blessed abundantly.

In the embrace of a loving community, you'll discover that you are not alone on your journey of faith. You'll find the strength to face life's challenges and the joy of celebrating life's victories together.

Today, take the first step in seeking community. Look for a church, small group or fellowship of believers where you can connect and grow

together. If you don't know where to start, pray and keep your eyes open as new opportunities for connection arise.

NOTES

Day 22

Mission: Possible

Luke 18:27: *Jesus replied,*
"What is impossible with man is possible with God."

In the realm of impossibilities, God's power shines most brilliantly. When all hope seems lost, when circumstances appear insurmountable, we find our unshakeable anchor of faith in the truth that, with God, absolutely nothing is impossible.

God is looking for those with whom He can do the impossible. What a pity that we plan only the things that we can do by ourselves. — **AW Tozer**

Luke captures this profound reality in Jesus' words: "What is impossible with man is possible with God."

Throughout Scripture we encounter countless stories of people and circumstances transformed by God – water parting, dead men rising, thousands being fed. These are miracles showcasing the magnificent power of God.

We do not often observe such amazing miracles today. We more often see God working in less dramatic ways on our behalf to bring us the help and protection we need. But sometimes we do not even notice God's work on our behalf.

As we face mountains of impossibility – no matter what they might be – we serve a God who delights in doing what seems impossible. His power is not bound by human limitations or the laws of nature.

And when God doesn't change our outward circumstances, His Spirit works to help us cope with them. His everlasting love is ever present, even when life is hard.

Faith doesn't deny the existence of obstacles or challenges. Instead, it recognizes that God's power is greater. He is able to bring us through those difficulties.

Today, when you feel overwhelmed or even before that, do these five things:

- ◆ *trust God's promises,*
- ◆ *seek His guidance,*
- ◆ *lean into His strength,*
- ◆ *surrender your doubts and fears, and*
- ◆ *embrace the truth that, with God, all things are possible.*

God is ready to turn your circumstances into a testimony of His power and faithfulness.

NOTES

Day 23

WHEN YOU REJOICE PEACE FOLLOWS

Philippians 4:4-7: *Rejoice in the Lord always. I will say it again: Rejoice! Let your gentleness be evident to all. The Lord is near. Do not be anxious about anything, but in every situation, by prayer and petition, with thanksgiving, present your requests to God. And the peace of God, which transcends all understanding, will guard your hearts and your minds in Christ Jesus.*

One of the greatest treasures found in Scripture surfaces in the last chapter of Philippians. While writing from a jail cell with the threat of possible death, the Apostle Paul thought it necessary to admonish other believers not to be anxious about anything.

> *A rejoicing heart soon makes a praising tongue.*
> - Charles Spurgeon

Peace may seem unattainable when we are in difficult circumstances, but it actually is within our reach. Paul offered a promise from God that quickens the Spirit of all believers across cultures, socioeconomic status and levels of maturity.

- ◆ Do you find yourself suffering anxiety?
- ◆ Do you find yourself fretting and unable to rest?
- ◆ Do you feel depressed?

Anxious people are often prayerless people.

Anxiety is the absence of peace. When we are anxious and in need of peace, we can gain peace from beyond ourselves. It comes from God. God's peace is beyond our understanding, but God makes it available to us. And this peace will guard our hearts and minds, even in anxious times.

The Apostle Paul does not say God's peace *may* guard us; he says God's peace *will* guard our hearts and minds. Paul presents an absolute statement, one full of certainty and hope. Our search for peace ends in Jesus.

Today, prayerfully submit your worries to God. Find the joy of letting God's majestic and divine peace replace all of your anxieties.

Let God's peace free you from the weight of your troubles. Let God's peace, not the anxieties of the world, control your life.

NOTES

Day 24

TRAGEDY NEED
NOT CRUSH YOU

Psalm 34:18: *The Lord is close to the brokenhearted and saves those who are crushed in spirit.*

Tragedy is an unwelcome visitor in our lives, a harsh and painful reality that can shake us to our core. It arrives uninvited, leaving behind a trail of tears, questions and brokenness.

Never let the presence of a storm cause you to doubt the presence of God.
- Craig Groeschel

It's often difficult to sense the Lord's presence when the pain of the present is so overwhelming.

But God is not a distant, detached observer of our suffering. He is close to us, intimately acquainted with our joys and our pains. He sees every tear, hears every cry and holds every shattered piece of our hearts.

Our tough times may help us to notice God's closeness to us. When life's struggles cause us to feel weak and lost, we often notice the closeness of God. The Lord is always near, but difficulties can help us experience this closeness.

Grief, pain and confusion may threaten to overwhelm us. But in the midst of our darkest hours, there is a promise that shines through – the Lord is near.

Consider the story of Job, a man who endured unimaginable tragedy. He lost his wealth, his health and his family. Yet, in the midst of his suffering, he clung to his faith and cried out to God.

Though tragedy may leave scars that never fully fade, it can also be a catalyst for a deeper, more profound faith. Through our brokenness, we can find a new understanding of God's grace, compassion and ability to bring beauty from ashes. In Him, we find hope even in the midst of life's most challenging circumstances.

Today, ask God to help you sense His presence. Ask Him to help you see beyond your problem. And then make a list, in thought or writing, of all the good that is happening in your life despite the difficulties. When you see your blessings you will see that God is with you.

NOTES

Day 25

TRUST GOD BEYOND YOUR UNDERSTANDING

Proverbs 3:5-6: *Trust in the Lord with all your heart and lean not on your own understanding; in all your ways submit to him, and he will make your paths straight.*

I n the tapestry of life, there are threads of joy, sorrow and uncertainty. Often, it's this last thread – the uncertainty of not understanding what God is doing – that challenges our faith the most.

"Never be afraid to trust an unknown future to a known God."
- Corrie ten Boom

We long for clear answers and a roadmap for our lives, but God's ways are often mysterious and beyond our comprehension.

Here, we find a powerful truth: While we may not understand what God is doing, we can trust in

His wisdom and His plan. This may sound cliche, but there is a profound sense of peace in placing your trust in the Almighty and Powerful Creator of the universe.

Trusting God is not always easy, but it is most certainly worth it.

◆ It requires a willingness to let go of our own desires and plans.

◆ It requires that we surrender control of our lives to Him.

◆ It requires us to step out in faith, even when we're unsure of the outcome.

As we do these things we experience His peace, His love and His faithfulness in ways we never thought possible.

In those moments when you grapple with the uncertainty of not understanding what God is doing, remember that your faith is being refined and your relationship with God is growing deeper.

Today, embrace the mystery, for it is often in the unknown that God's greatest work is done. As you trust in Him with all your heart, you will find that even when you don't understand His ways you can rest in the assurance that He is leading you on a path that ultimately brings glory to His name and blessing to your life.

NOTES

Day 26

THANKFULNESS IS YOUR MYSTERIOUS TEACHER

1 Thessalonians 5:18: *... give thanks in all circumstances; for this is God's will for you in Christ Jesus."*

I t is easy to give thanks when everything is going well. It is altogether different when our situations stink. In those dark times, thankfulness does not come easily.

"No matter what our circumstances, we can find a reason to be thankful."
–Dr. David Jeremiah

The Apostle Paul often spoke of giving thanks to God. He did so even though he had been beaten, persecuted and thrown into prison.

Paul, despite his conditions, found ways to give thanks to God. He had discovered a profound and magnificent truth – gratitude and thankfulness have a way of delivering peace to the person giving it regardless of the external forces.

Gratitude is the instrument God has given to us to defeat the depravity and wretchedness of self-loathing, hardships and strongholds. Not only is it beneficial, it is the will of God.

Thankfulness transforms the mind and condition of those who joyfully choose it.

Gratitude ...

- ◆ ... turns wounds into worship,
- ◆ ... changes difficulties into demonstrations,
- ◆ ... transforms trials into testimonies and
- ◆ ... uses storms for gloriously divine surprises.

Today presents you with an opportunity. Whatever you are going through, you have the opportunity to learn the joy and power of thankfulness. It is a mysterious teacher waiting to take root in your life. Choose to be thankful today, not begrudgingly but authentically. As you do, let the Spirit of God bring healing to you and whatever you are facing.

NOTES

Day 27

YOU MAY LOOK TO A BRIGHTER FUTURE

Romans 8:18: I consider that our present sufferings are not worth comparing with the glory that will be revealed in us.

As a Christian, it can be difficult to reconcile the struggles of this life with the hope we have in Christ. We long for peace and comfort, yet so often we find ourselves entrenched in hardship and trial.

The future is as bright as the promises of God.
- William Carey

In tough times, it's easy for our faith to waiver as we struggle to see beyond the present pain. However, in the midst of earthly suffering, there is also great hope – one based on a heavenly promise of something far greater than we can imagine.

We look to a brighter future full of joy knowing that God's unconditional love is present with us even now.

We don't always understand why God allows us to go through such difficulties and sorrows, but we know He works everything for our ultimate good (Romans 8:28).

No matter what challenges we face – illness, grief or loss – His love for us is unwavering, and His plans for our lives are perfect.

The Apostle Paul reminds us in Romans 8:18 that our sufferings are nothing compared to the glory that will be revealed in us. This means the hardships we endure in this life, though painful, are only temporary. They pale in comparison to the eternal joy and bliss we will experience in the presence of God.

Let's not lose heart when we face trials of various kinds.

Today, if you're going through a difficult season, remember that this too shall pass. You are not alone in your suffering, and God is working all things together for good. Hold onto the hope of eternity, and let it carry you through the hardships of today.

NOTES

Day 28

YOU CAN TRUST GOD

Numbers 23:19: *"God is not human, that he should lie, not a human being, that he should change his mind. Does he speak and then not act? Does he promise and not fulfill?"*

In a world where words are sometimes fleeting and promises easily broken, it's a profound comfort to know that God, in His divine nature, is unwavering in His promises. God is trustworthy.

"Every single thing He has ever or will ever say is true. The simplicity of faith is this: taking God's Word for it." — Jackie Hill Perry

Our lives are filled with promises – by loved ones, leaders, ourselves. But how often do these promises go unfulfilled? How often are they broken, either due to human frailty or changing circumstances?

In contrast, God's promises are steadfast and true. His words are not empty or idle; they are filled with divine purpose and certainty.

When God speaks a promise, it is as good as done. His promises are permanently and undeniably stamped with a seal of unfailing love and faithfulness.

In our lives, we encounter situations that seem impossible or that challenge our faith. It's in these moments that we can hold fast to the promises of God. His promises are like anchors for our souls, providing stability and hope amid life's uncertainties.

Today, take a moment to consider the promises God has made to you in His Word – promises of love, grace, forgiveness and eternal life. Promises of His presence, His guidance and His provision. Rest in these unchanging promises of God. They are a testament to His character – faithful, true and forever reliable. And as you trust Him, you'll find strength and comfort.

NOTES

Day 29

GOD CALLS YOU TO PRESS ON

Philippians 3:13-14: Brothers and sisters, I do not consider myself yet to have taken hold of it. But one thing I do: Forgetting what is behind and straining toward what is ahead, I press on toward the goal to win the prize for which God has called me heavenward in Christ Jesus.

The Apostle Paul, faced numerous difficulties and hardships, including persecution and imprisonment. In his letter to the Philippians he offers us a powerful example of pressing on. "Forgetting what is behind and straining toward what is ahead, I press on toward the goal."

Getting over a painful experience is much like crossing monkey bars. You have to let go at some point in order to move forward.
- C. S. Lewis

In our lives, it's easy to become bogged down by past mistakes, regrets, difficulties or missed opportunities. We may carry the burdens of yesterday into today, hindering our progress and joy.

Paul reminds us we must intentionally choose to forget what is behind. That doesn't mean erasing our memories; it means releasing the grip the past may have on our hearts and minds.

Pressing on is not about avoiding challenges or pretending difficulties don't exist.

It's about recognizing that, despite our circumstances, we have a heavenly calling and a divine purpose.

It's about straining toward the goal with perseverance and determination, fueled by the knowledge that God is with us.

Today, release the grip of the past, strain toward what lies ahead and press on with unwavering faith. Trust that the prize God has called you to is worth the effort and know that He walks beside you, empowering you to overcome every obstacle.

NOTES

Day 30

FIND JOY BEYOND
YOUR CIRCUMSTANCES

Habakkuk 3:17-18:
Though the fig tree does not bud
and there are no grapes on the vines,
though the olive crop fails
and the fields produce no food,
though there are no sheep in the pen
and no cattle in the stalls,
yet I will rejoice in the Lord,
I will be joyful in God my Savior.

Habukkuk vividly describes a dire situation where nothing seems to be going right. The fig tree isn't budding, the vines have no grapes, the olive crop has failed and there's a shortage of food and livestock.

> *"Joy is not necessarily the absence of suffering, it is the presence of God."*
> - Sam Storms

In other words, it's a scene of absolute desolation and despair. Nothing seems to be going well.

Yet, in the midst of these bleak circumstances, Habakkuk makes a profound declaration: "Yet I will rejoice in the Lord, I will be joyful in God my Savior."

His joy isn't contingent on a bountiful harvest or an abundance of blessings; his joy is anchored in his relationship with God.

True joy transcends circumstances. It's a joy rooted in the knowledge that God is present and faithful, even when our external world seems to crumble.

This concept of joy despite hardship is one that can be challenging to comprehend and even more difficult to practice. Our natural tendency is to equate our level of joy with the amount of comfort or pleasure we experience in life. Nevertheless, true delight comes not from our circumstances but from God.

Today, no matter what circumstances you face, remember that joy is available to you through your relationship with God. Just like Habakkuk, you can declare that you will rejoice in the Lord and be joyful in God your Savior even when everything else seems to be falling apart.

NOTES

About the Author

Mikey Osborne is a pastor, Christ-follower, husband and father. He writes a lot, speaks a lot, and eats a lot. His desire is to see the church awakened to the reality of the Gospel and actively engage their mind and their communities for the kingdom of God. He writes underneath the shadows of East Texas pines while serving as the Missions and Disciple Outreach Coordinator for Texans on Mission.

About Texans on Mission

Founded as Texas Baptist Men, Texan on Mission empowers Christian volunteers to take on the biggest challenges around the globe, changing the world one act of service at a time. Since 1967, Texans on Mission volunteers have delivered help, hope and healing to millions of hurting people and raised up the next generation to do likewise. Texans on Mission has helped start and train disaster relief groups in all 50 states, giving birth to the third-largest disaster relief network in the nation.

TEXANSONMISSION.ORG

OTHER RESOURCES

 MAKE
LIFE
COUNT

 HOLY
INTERRUPTIONS

 REWRITING
FATHERS

 FAMILY
MINISTRY
THAT COUNTS

 HOLY
INTERRUPTIONS
MISSION PREP GUIDE
& JOURNAL

Made in the USA
Columbia, SC
26 May 2025

58185399R00063